PILGRIM EYE

Mary L. Junge

For June –
All good wishes to you.
Thanks for joining us at
the downtown Library.
All of life is a poem.
— Mary Junge

LAUREL
POETRY
COLLECTIVE

ACKNOWLEDGEMENTS

The author wishes to thank the editors of the publications in which some of the poems in this volume were previously published: "Georgia Saw the Blue Line" in *Pulling for Good News* (Laurel Poetry Collective, 2004); "Early Signs" in Mary L. Junge, *Express Train* (Pudding House Publications, 2002); "Staying in the Light" in *Minnesota Poetry Calendar*; "Dust," "Faces of Motherhood," and "Why We Have Two Hundred Photos of Italy and Few Have Captions" in *Water~Stone*; "Sleepwalker" in *Sidewalks* and *Express Train*; "Simplicity" in *Express Train*; "Letter from Gala to Salvador Dalí" in *ArtWord Quarterly*; "In Consideration of Things" in *Hunger Enough* (Pudding House Publications, 2004); "Ars Poetica" in *A New Name for the Sun* (Laurel Poetry Collective, 2003).

"Persuasion" was set to letterpress broadside by Nancy Walden, Laurel Poetry Collective, 2003.

A passage from the poem "One Train May Hide Another" by Kenneth Koch (in *One Train* [Alfred A. Knopf, 1994]) appears in "Simplicity"; a passage from the poem "Space Is the Wake of Time" by Paul Zweig (in *Eternity's Woods* [Wesleyan University Press, 1985]) appears in "What We Mean to Be Today."

———

In gratitude to Mark and my family; a constellation of supportive friends; the Café Con Amore poetry group; the Laurel Poetry Collective; my spiritual community at the First Universalist Church of Minneapolis; and those who assisted with the details of this manuscript: Pam Wynn, Nolan Zavoral, Margot Galt, Ilze Mueller, Sylvia Ruud, and mentors Roseann Lloyd and Deborah Keenan.

© 2004 by Mary L. Junge

Printed in the United States of America.

Published by LAUREL POETRY COLLECTIVE
1168 Laurel Avenue, St. Paul MN 55104
www.laurelpoetry.com

Book design by Sylvia Ruud

Library of Congress Cataloging-in-Publication Data

Junge, Mary.
    Pilgrim eye / by Mary Junge.
        p. cm.
    ISBN 0-9728934-8-2
    I. Title.
PS3610.U54P55 2004
811'.6--dc22

                            2004008278

for my mother

CONTENTS

Blue

Yellow

Red

Blue

GEORGIA SAW THE BLUE LINE

slit of a doorway
into the tunnel
where souls traverse
to their final cradles.
Georgia saw
the lighter sky
beyond,
so she didn't have to hurry,
could luxuriate
in the pockets of bliss,
could feed her third,
ecstatic pilgrim eye
from her bulging
sack of colors.

THE UNSEEN

The thought growing and the distant hungry—
The flea, the louse, the microbe.
The disease that hides until treatment is useless.
The prayer, an instant cry that stops the train in time,
And the one that couldn't stop.
The love that keeps the child from
Joining, and the loved child who joins.
The animal you would choose anytime,
And the other animal you were assigned at birth.
The fire you try to limit despite terrible winds,
And the distant fires—of forest, of oil moving on water.
The flowering plant you water before it shows green.
The cocoon—of plain moth or bright
Blue butterfly—you'll never know which.
The prize you regretted giving away—
And the one you wish you had given.
The dream that knows all you seek and
Wakes you—
And the dream that refuses.
The day you return to, repeating its anguish,
And hunger hovering like rain.
The cells mutating,
And the vicious cells devoured by the good.
The chaos and the pockets of order we try to make.
The whole world of it, invisible.
Yet you believe. You do believe.

Dream Narrative

Story without language, for instance.
Endless walk through a city you visited long ago.
The long, unreturned kiss that insists.
You know the morning,
The one to which you cannot wake,
Your dream more compelling than your life

With everything suddenly before you as in a perfect map

Until you lose your glasses.
Blind, you must feel your way,
As you do each day.
So you wake to your life.

THOUGH THERE IS NO WIND, YOUR ORANGE KITE LIFTS

It stays with you and remains elsewhere too,
Gravitates to all that is true,
Cures the ache the doctor cannot,
Will not wither or sicken,
Sends every message in the beak of a bird.
Shows you how to live with your hunger after
The fields have burned.

You tell no one of the dream and
What it foretold.
Your torn edges sew themselves:
Your strange separateness fades.
You forget your obsession with locks—
Forget what you could lose,
Fall into a crack of time—
Freedom. Fear is a planet in a distant galaxy.
You untie the safety ropes,
Swim fast above the undertow,
Pet the stray cat.
As if bread, you offer your body to your lover.

White Weasel

You spy a white weasel,
Its small eyes fixed on yours.

You remember the child you were,
How you gave yourself over to snow,
How you pressed your back into the layers,
Fluff, crust, inches of old,

And below that, the frozen ground.
You filled your bare hands,
Licked it first, then ate mouthful after mouthful:
You wanted to be snow.

Lying still, you pretended to be invisible,
Anonymous as a snowflake,
Then moved your arms up and down,
Up and down, as if you were flying, and then

You remained still for a long time, stood up gingerly,
Tiptoed out and away from the print
Of an angel, whose wings (your secret wings)
Would soon be hidden under a dusting of new snow.

EARLY SIGNS

At the lake, our hair bleached whiter
every day—*towheads* they called us.
Already I sensed the coiling
in my sister's head.

Our permanent teeth had come in: she refused to brush.
Our whitened hair grew fast: she refused to comb.
Our faces were blackened with soot after evening bonfires:
she refused to wash.

Sometimes she could not hear me.
Only the flames spoke to her,
or the rhythm of waves lapping,
or the fine sand that stuck to her needful fingers.

When my friends and I wanted penny candy,
we sneaked off without her,
to walk the mile
to the Little Store.

Now, she spends her long days inside.
Her drab brown hair never lightens. All day long
she chews on used thoughts while deepening the narrow
circular path around herself.

WORK ETHIC

Father takes me with him to the appliance store
After closing time. I find the adding machine
In the tiny, dark office at the back of the store—
Where the numbers never add up
To the profit Mother says we need.

Front windows in the showroom look like black holes,
Though I know Main Street must be on the other side.
In rare places a shine glances from the white stoves and refrigerators—
1960 marvels. Here is where he spends his days
Only steps away from Potter's Bar where he goes after locking up.

Mother says he talks too much but can't close a deal.
Morie, on hourly wage, spends his days here too, between
The tall Frigidaires so much nicer than our own—
Yet exactly like the one he took home to his grateful wife
Six months earlier, never paying a dime toward what was due.

I grow a small knot of pity for my father,
Knowing finally how he must weave among the appliances
Each dull morning—each dull afternoon
While the business his dead father started is slowly
Falling off the edge of the map.

VORTEX

Under the giant roving eye they look like dolls.
Unwarned, they move freely:
A woman drives to buy a bottle of milk.
A man paints a fence.
An elderly couple weeds the flower garden.
The town dogs begin to howl in unison.
The greenish sky turns itself inside out,
Revealing its thick lining of deep purple.

At the edge of town a woman
Carries her swaddled baby from car to house.
Lifted skyward, together at first,
They are assigned different orbits.

My father, a volunteer for the fire department,
Finds the woman unconscious, miles from where
Her ride began. Her body is unbruised—
Perfect but for the thousands of slivers of wood
Lodged in her flesh.

Still swaddled in the same blanket,
Baby has been set down on the other side of town.
A whole day passes before they are reunited:
No one thinks to match the unharmed baby
With the wailing woman with a million slivers.

IN THE QUIET HOUSES

In the silent moments of predawn,
In the salt and pepper shakers on stoves
In the dark kitchens,
In the sleeping books on hard shelves
In dens and bedrooms,
In the curtains that absorb
Our exhalations,
Behind our fluttering eyelids
Comes the dream:

We are rising in our nightshirts.
We are floating toward the same small bird.
We are standing under stars with our neighbors.
No one is cold or hungry.
We hold hands.
We raise our faces to the moon.
We begin together a chorus in a low hum.

Inside the Glass House

for Vicky

The greenhouse warms us after our long bike ride
on this first cold day of September

You confess that many days you are lonely.
On those days, you must call me, I say.

A gigantic glass fish is poised,
as if jumping from its small square pond.

A young girl tugs on her grandmother's hand,
What is it?

An attendant pushes a mobile bed inside.
The woman on it gapes at the fish.

Another woman stands frozen,
her eyes fixed on her hands

(she reminds me of my sister
who also lives in that other world).

I confess that some days I am confused
by the speed and muchness of my life.

It's as if zebras are stampeding through my head.
Those are the days you must call me, you say.

Four different types of lilies grow in the pond,
but none is in bloom.

There are no real fish—no carp, not even goldfish—in the pool.
A sign says: *Do Not Eat the Oranges, Pesticides Have Been Applied.*

For a long time we sit together in the quiet.
We look at the fish, the lilies, the woman on the bed,

and the woman fixed on her hands. As we're leaving,
you stoop to read the name of the Bombay purple celosias.

Some days I am lost in the blur of zebras.
Many days you are lonely.

LOVE BECOMES RELIGION

for Ralph

Days like this I rewind
The film of his death, make him
Fly back through the hospital window,
Return him to his small room, then walk him
Through the locked doors,
Out of the hospital,
Into the open,
Where I let him enter,
Again, the dangerous world.
Only this time there is love:
Love flows in the rivers.
Love blooms in the center of the flowers.
Love is in the air we breathe.
And it is the love that
Kills the desperate ache
In his heart
So he lives.
This time he goes right on living.

NINE MINERS TRAPPED SEVENTY-SEVEN HOURS

July 24, 2002, Somerset, Pennsylvania

If we could hold them as they were when napping,
Their heads resting against each other
As women would,
Or warming each other,
Death's cloak widening in the water below,
Or carrying water to one another,
Having found this perfect use for hands.

If we could keep their faces
As they were emerging from the shaft,
Darkened with soot, bright with surprise,
Facing the daylight as if newborns,

If we could freeze them in these slivers of hope,
Our hearts stretched with anonymous love,
Not as the newspaper describes them a year later,
Anxious and depressed, only two working,
Then we might seem like a people worth saving,
Every one of us worth the struggle of each long day.

WHAT WE MEAN TO BE TODAY

for Paul Zweig

We stand as *garlands of pure place*—
Home—while the lake remains empty and
Ready as an adolescent womb.
Three lifeguards, in their red shorts and
Crosses, form a triangle on the empty beach:
The graduates will not enter this water today.

Hidden are the dark petals we slip into their future—
Today we mean only to avoid casting shadows.
Today we mean to be all they need,
So they can leave us, so they can glide
Into the shimmering future, the chosen,
(As we once were)

To correct Earth's wrong trajectory.

To Be Ready

Waking, then falling back into dreams,
Each time sinking deeper,
Not swimming, as usual, toward daylight.
Each time turning the cheek from morning,
Each blurred waking
Turning again toward the exquisite darkness,
Toward the repeating, ever changing dream—
Dream with a heartbeat all its own,
The way it must be when dying,
When one is ready to give up the earth.
The way it must be when one is ready.

Yellow

STAYING IN THE LIGHT

Morning light made dew on the grass silver.
Afternoons I set my newborn
up to the front window where he
could drink up sun to cure his jaundice.
Next to his dewy skin, mine looked used, wrinkled.
Stormy evenings after light parted the sky,
we startled at the loud afterthought—thunder.

We still startle at the loud afterthought, thunder,
stormy evenings when light splits the sky.
We are not afraid. It's only angels bowling,
while we grow older. Tomorrow morning
the sun will come again. We will drink it
like newborns set up to the front window.
There will be dew on the grass, on the silver grass.

Dust

for C. D. Wright

Why should you believe that I was
The poet of children?
Poet of fumblings and accidents
(Who perhaps overused the emergency room
As a setting),
Whose images smelled of clean laundry—
And sometimes backseat vomit?
That I was the poet of large black pots and pans,
Basil and garlic, geraniums and
The commonest of our Midwest perennials—
Coneflower and clematis,
Poet who gardened and baked
After the mothers who owned Palm Pilots
Had returned to their offices and schools,
Poet left to oversee the lemonade stands
With the neighborhood nannies.

Do not judge me harshly.
I was handed this particular, simple life.
Anyway, wasn't I also the poet
Who listened to desperate stories—
Like yours?
Who made noodle casseroles for the broken
And kept believing that stories could save us—
Kept believing in language—
After the exotic topics and perfect metaphors
Were already overused or assigned to others?
And didn't I watch the flowers from our gardens
Open in summer? And didn't I set out suet
For our birds in winter?
And wasn't mine the door

On which your children rapped
After you'd promised them fresh cookies—
After you'd started and stopped and said, *Go
Borrow a cup of sugar?*

Visiting My Sister in the Psychiatric Ward

Their eyes offer something—pity, I suppose.
They are like the others, with no cure.

Thank you, I say when they give her room number.
(But why three of them?)

The children and I walk the long dirty blue carpet.
Her door is first on the right. I am grateful to round

the sharp corner and step out of the nurses' view.
She lies in her narrow bed, greets us with a weak smile, sits up.

Her son goes to her. The primal code between them
sends a shudder through me. Eleven now,

he sits close to her, his feet dangling
from the high bed, his eyes locked with hers.

She rubs circles on his leg.
No bridge, knife, razor, rope, belt, gun, pills, car,

speeding traffic, poison, fire, window, or sharp glass.
Only words of death, and tears, so many tears.

There are mothers who do worse than threaten suicide.
Yes, there are worse things a mother could do.

SLEEPWALKER

after Emil Nolde, painter, 1857–1956

You guess she is from the underworld,
the way she hovers above the ground,
pulled by a hand you can't see.

Her face is pale,
her blackened
lips pulled downward.

The moon steps out of its circle
as she begins waltzing
with a partner.

You could swear you read her thoughts
when they spill onto your pillow.
Other nights, too, you got drunk

from watching her—and from trains
screaming down your back
as you moaned into your pillow.

Dawn finds you dog tired,
in your motel bed, next to your wife.
Everything floods back: the hand in your dream,

reaching for the young ones. Knock on the door—
middle of the night—your wife warns,
Don't answer it—peering through the peephole—

your son stares back, bewildered, too,
half-naked in night shorts—the pale face,
darkened lips filling negative space now.

So you throw open the door and shout,
What are you doing out there?—
I don't know, he mutters, *but let me in.*

By the Yellow Roses

I join the men in plush leather chairs.
I join the men who close their eyes
To shoppers' jangle,
Until there is only the music
Floating from the nook under the *up* escalator.
The years of piano lessons have paid off.
We are captivated:
Holiday shoppers with tired feet.

What if we let the music be the main thing?

But we don't—maybe can't, I don't know.
When we open our eyes,
The people on the escalators make a psychedelic X
Behind the pianist's head.
We can't look, close our eyes again.
If only I could clap after each song.
The pianist, too, knows his role.
He rarely looks up.
He only sighs after each piece,
Then continues, his right foot gently
Pressing the pedal at the correct times—
Lingering for each correct count.
It seems I have been here for hours.
I should be going, I think to him
Between the notes floating in my head.
So much to do. The appointment later.
I want to say *goodbye*—and *thank you*
Out loud
Yet it seems wrong to interrupt—
And wrong *not* to

After all he has given.
I press my swollen feet back into shoes
Before walking out, like the bitter one
With the habit of using, then jilting, her lovers.

SIMPLICITY

for Kenneth Koch

I'd like to be easy, to will him into the larger world—
Poland this first time far away.
At the gate, my lips brush his cheek lightly before

He walks into the belly of the plane. From the airport,
I drive to my sister's to deliver her birthday gift,
A rolling grocery cart, from our father.

She is waiting for me, perched on the front steps
Of her apartment building in the still heat
Of midsummer with Miss Blossom

Who lives in the building across the street—
And who uses her false teeth to carefully chew cashews.
My sister, nearly fifty, has never left the country,

Has never flown in an airplane.
Miss Blossom has not traveled far either I guess.
I can't help but imagine—

There must have been a time
When we were small—
A moment, an hour, a day—even a week,

When I wasn't looking,
When everything changed. Wood ducks fall
From their nests into water (safely)

Twenty-four hours after hatching.
I have kept this son close for thirteen years.
Sometimes one grief hides another.

I'd like to call mine a mother's pure grief—
A common trial of letting go.
Why, I wonder, can't a moment remain simple,

Be just what it seems to be,
Without drawing out the shadows of the past?
Instead, one dream can easily hide another,

Or can hide a nightmare—like the one
Where I look away and turn back,
Then begin searching for what is not there.

A Lecture on Loons

We walked a path through thick woods.
Loons. Beautiful trilling.
My husband en route to another hospital:
Loons, my welcome distraction.
The babies rode on their mothers' backs I think.
Stayed together as a family somehow—
Or not. Nested precariously in weeds maybe.
Disturbed by noise, especially boats.
Nesting sites decreasing. Yes.
A different song for everything. Facts like mist.

Like the drive to the first hospital, where they took
Images no one there could read.
Next hospital, one hundred miles.
They would find nothing: I had to believe it,
Had to listen about loons even if the ranger's
Facts appeared and flickered out, like falling stars.
Not think of negative possibilities,
Not foresee a helicopter flying toward a neurosurgeon.
Impossible now, to be sure of any of it,
Except the warble a mother loon makes when distressed,
The sound I can imitate perfectly.

FACES OF MOTHERHOOD

1. *Circle*

I've become a small bright sun
with three children orbiting.
They trust me, fools,
to keep them on course.

How will they go on
when they discover
I have nothing to give—
but love?
Some days even *that*
shines in muted colors,
rises in hushed,
garbled sounds
no one
can understand.

Don't look to me for answers
my little bablets.
I only know how to pray.

2. *Waiting for Spring*

I try to imagine green or
my own forgiveness.

3. *Age Six*

In my dog Snoopy's
only litter,
there was a runt
my parents
sent to the bottom

of the Sheyenne River
with a large rock
in a burlap sack while I pleaded,

Don't do it.
They called it *the kindest act*.
What if I too have a killing side?

4. *Nursing*

My own children took to the breast
easily. My nipples tingle
when I see a woman
nursing her baby.
How mine sucked
with such strength!

Loving them gave me such
happiness, I wanted to give myself
away. Nights I couldn't
sleep enough, I dragged
my limp body into the
half-light, pulled my
shadow for the baby's life.

My death seemed small.

5. *Evil*

I worry when they're out at night. I try, but fail,
to give them over to the world gently—without my fears.

The oldest is lost in his frenzy and
need to block out daylight, to plunge into

oblivion, down the dark hole of
liquor that sucked down his grandfather.

I won't release him.

6. *Waiting for Spring*

I try to imagine green
or my own forgiveness.

7. *Dream*

A woman hands me a wash bucket,
tears the book from my hands,
gives me a vacuum cleaner for my birthday,
holds out a gold coin, walks
backward while I follow.

I always follow.

She murmurs, *You were only the vessel*,
teaches my children
to cry in the tone that used to
make my milk let down.

8. *Advice*

Wait until your kids are grown.

9. *Energy*

Important parts of me
disappear.

When my mother-in-law
suggests I sew,

I see that
my hands are gone.

I go out for new shoes,
but my feet, too, have disappeared.

If my mother were alive,
I'd be a better mother.

When she died, her overworked heart
simply stopped like a clock that had unwound.

10. *Waiting for Spring*

I try to imagine green
or my own forgiveness

11. *Deferred Needs*

Desires for chocolate,
sex, clothing I don't need
are all I can name.
Greed can't be satisfied. Possessions—

dozens of pairs of shoes,
twenty-some scarves,
blouses, skirts, pants and dresses
will be useless
to my children as they
deliver them to the thrift store.
Will they complain then, of my tendency
to collect and hoard?

12. *Progeny*

How I'd raise my children
if they were

girls! I'd teach them about
beauty and grace.

But I live in a foreign country.

13. *Forgiveness*

Now I forgive
my mother her
imperfections, rub the
pearls between my fingers
dusky mornings.

14. *Andrew Turns Eight*

His smile opens up the world
again this morning.
He's doing homework,
regrouping and carrying,
printing a tiny 1 to
represent every set of 10.
Soon he'll know the
real meaning of subtraction,
how someone
can be taken
just as you're about to grasp
singular love.

I'm busy watching
his thick eyelashes

brush over his lovely cheeks.
Don't remind me of patterns and
chaos theory.

15. *Song*

Now I add more yellow to the stars,
release my own hand—the one

that grips the gown of all that has
slipped away into the night.

CHANT OF THE SCHOOL LUNCH LADIES

for the lottery winners in Holdingford, Minnesota

The lottery will not change my life they say
Scooping the mashed potatoes with renewed zest,
Pouring the tan gravy into the hole in the middle.
O mark, O krone, peseta, euro.
O slot machine winnings.
Who cares if our salary is worth our salt?
O crashing coins, where were you
When our children needed everything new?
O honey pot, O pot at rainbow's end,
Don't change us too much, please.
O do barter, barter with us now.
When can we give up the old cars for new?
O we will keep pouring the gravy,
Thick and warm into the little craters we make
With the back of a spoon.
Remember? Remember the money changers sent away?
O but no, we are not money changers.

Day 2: One lunch lady calls in sick,
Doesn't want to smash potatoes today.
O not today the gravy. Maybe tomorrow. O no, say the rest,
We've lost one. There she goes.
O peso, shilling, dollar, taka. O franc, dinar, pula, pound.
O mint, O whales' teeth, cattle, cowrie shells.
Will the lottery change my life?
O funny money, shekel, won, yen.
O peso, lira gone forever.
Whose picture is on the money now? Not Caesar's
Say the lunch ladies in unison.
Say the ladies loudly:
The lottery will not change *my* life. Not *mine*.
O no. O no. Not money.

EACH DAY

Called back to the river of my body,
My grown son clings to me

And alternately pulls away. Then he
Laughs at my need to embrace.

See how the old floor curves
As if to warn of danger?

See how the door hangs from its hinges
As if it is falling?

Listen:

Now that two of my children are grown,
Each day I imagine them

As happy, kind men far away.
Each day I imagine them

Out of reach
Of danger's clawed hands.

What Makes a Bird a Bird?

Not beauty: Think of the crow, large and clumsy—
Now blamed for the robin's decline.

Not feathers: Consider the woman's dress in the late 1800s—
Made of thousands of Brazilian hummingbird feathers.

Not music: The songbird's music often scatters to wind.
Not goodness: The parasitic cowbird has two hundred hosts.

Not fearlessness: The babies in our birdfeeder-turned-nest
Didn't want to leave—practiced flying inside until we removed their roof.

The harried mother returned always, with a squirming green worm:
Her young screeched louder when they heard her land,

So she'd sit a few moments before going in—as I used to pause,
Resting my forehead on the wooden door outside baby's room—

While I gathered the best of myself,
Before I turned the door handle and went inside.

As the Map Tears

We turn to borders guarded—
To those who made rubble of our towers—

Who left children forever without.
How to answer now that we've been drawn

Into an old religious war,
Now that the winds of our country

Taste of iron and hatred?
We turn our fearful eyes skyward,

Think *explosion* as we pump gas,
Blood at the sight of strawberries,

Hands bound when we touch the clothesline.
The letter becomes omen,

Ring of the telephone   signal,
Knock on the door   trap.

Here I work from memory grown vague,
And an old-fashioned word: forgiveness.

Can it be true? The crows still caw,
And newborns still root at their mothers' breasts,

That world of flesh and sweet milk.
Aren't we starved for the milk

Of forgiveness—given and received—
The sole remedy for our hungry, shrinking hearts?

PANTOUM FOR PEACE

We build a vocabulary of faith.
Stop the bombs from falling.
We braid the rope of peace.
The children beg us to fry their catch, sunfish.

Stop the bombs from falling.
Idle minds fall easily into melancholy.
Fry our sunfish, our catch, beg the children.
Though hungry, we throw back our fish.

Melancholy keeps us idle.
A child believes all will be well if we say it.
We throw back our fish, still hungry.
We want to be faithful, like children.

Because we say it, a child believes it.
To say it, we must believe it.
We want to be like children, faithful.
Love alone makes the spinning world constant.

To believe it, we must say it.
Every small life matters.
The spinning world sometimes pauses for love.
Like tarnish on silver, we love the evil out of the world.

Even my small life matters.
When we hold the rope of peace, we must not let go.
We love the evil out of the world like tarnish on silver.
Every pulse reaches the ocean.

When we hold the rope of peace, we must not let go.
We braid the rope of peace.
Each pulse rides the ocean to the other side.
We build a vocabulary of faith.

Not Your Turn Yet

That's why.

Is it true what they say, nothing valuable washes up on the beach?
Don't the polished rocks and the shells count?

I like to think of myself as an agate—
Each year, each new grief polishing me smoother.
I like to think of my years as the thin stripes
Darkening in water, their beauty unnamed,
My core unharmed, protected in some essential way.

But how could a stone be hungry every day?

Last time at the ocean, while out for a morning walk,
A man tried to convert me to his religion.
Why did I let him walk beside me
After he'd asked what I thought of eternal salvation?
You can live forever, he assured me, so certain of all he had to offer—

In the same way that our president
Sent troops to liberate the people of Iraq.

YELLOW GHAZAL

for Adrienne Rich

In the cracks and hollows of summer's embrace
yellow sifts in, settles for its fleeting life—

not bright sun yellow, but the milky yellow
of late afternoon, pale yellow of a lemon's interior,

color of the ribbon I had long ago when I was a girl
who bought hair ribbons to match every outfit,

ribbons cut to eighteen inches on the wooden yardstick
nailed to the counter at the fabric store.

Ribbons kept the hair out of my eyes,
yes, and that girl suspected their color

mattered—she knew for certain
that texture and the sheen of things

dare us to save them, the way we stop
home movies when we suddenly

see ourselves there, on the screen, making
merry—the way we cling to summer.

Red

PERSUASION

The red hibiscus surprises
On this eighteenth day of October.
It does not know I meant to let it die—
That I decided to stop watering it in September—
That three frost warnings
Did not convince me to cover it—
That I wanted to be finished with it

And its mess—
Did not want to bring it inside
Where it would become
My winter obligation.
But the sun burned hot
Coaxing open a single red bloom,
Economical as a sudden kiss.

SNAKE TIME

There is a time when it's not quite spring, when the sun rises
especially for the snakes who've wound themselves together,
like the yarn balls knitters make in winter, in this cold place.
The snakes have stayed so close—too cold even for sex—and
stayed that way all winter, rotating inside out, outside in, to
share the warmth of their center before bulging from the ground
as a single round creature with dozens of heads bobbing, dozens
of tongues projecting, before they disassemble, before they slide
off to be alone, to prepare for the quietest mating dance of all.

The Common Lilac

Likes living on the edge of zone 3.
Its name a misnomer:
Nothing common about its look or smell
When it blooms briefly in late May,
When lavender boughs hang heavy,
When it droops and spills over our newly greened lawns,
When taking from a neighbor's hedge is not stealing,
When the time it takes to fill a vase becomes critical.

Later, in the still heat of summer,
After the lilac's perfume is nowhere,
If not absorbed by the cotton yarns of memory,
It wears the same simple green dress every day.
And we like it like that too.
In winter, it goes perfectly naked,
So we fondly call it dormant.

We wait for its purple, its perfume,
Find that lilac remains with us long after
Its tiny flowers have dried and blown.
We study old words:
Always, forever.

At Ding Darling in June

Today, so many crabs moved in the dead heat,
It seemed the roots of the mangroves were moving.

We lazily watched the casts of a lone boy fishing
Until our eyes discovered the alligator, eyes set on him.

Buoys mark the sandbars, but the sandbars
Shift according to wind and wake.

When we were kids, we liked to name everything
Dead or alive.

Were chickens still alive when they ran around
After their heads had been taken?

Were worms alive after we'd cut them into tiny pieces?
Now that I can see my youth at a distance,

Still quivering and warm, is it
Too late now, to recover the nights and love I wasted?

Reasons to Live in Minnesota

People don't realize all the things that can kill ya right here in Minnesota, but we don't have half-a-what they got in other states—no poisonous snakes, no scorpions, hardly nothin' like that except for the brown recluse spider. If you get bit by it, it bores a big hole that gets weepy real fast—and the infection can go straight down to the bone. One bite can kill ya. And there's the cockroach. Most folks don't even know we got 'em here. That's why I ask for plastic, not paper at the grocery store. They love paper bags and the food and moisture on the checkout counters. Even the so-called harmless snakes can about kill ya. Once my sister-in-law was in the hospital for two weeks after a garden snake bit her. They're not poisonous, but their mouths are so full of bacteria, they can give ya a nasty infection. Most people don't know it, but every fall, a buck gores some guy to death as he's walking out to get the mail.

I could recall only one story to tell the pest control worker who had befriended me in the tire store. It was impressive though —about the crows attacking and killing the elderly in Beijing. But no—the Orkin man wasn't finished. He could top that.

A couple of years ago, right here in Minnesota, an old man was fishing and got too close to a swan's nest. The mother dove at him and knocked him clean outta his boat and he drowned. Still, we don't have half-a-what they gotta put up with in other states.

GARNET

1.

Turn me one way, I shimmer—
another, I am dried blood.
This way an elf—that way
a buffalo. Like this, fire—

like that, cold ash.
Look, I am the smooth rose—
blink, I am purslane.
Up, ropes stretching—

down, night slacking.
Twist, a garter snake—
turn, a rattler.
Here, my finger beckons—

there, my hand motions halt.
Can you feel my blood,
warm and dark,
the pleasure of extremes?

So many colors pile one
on top of another, behind
the richness of black. This stone
should have a door, a place to rest my eyes.

It hypnotizes, urges my
fingers to turn it around,
search
for the beginning.

2.

Watching a friend eat octopus, I saw
the slippery pile gleam from her plate.
She bent her head as she worked at it,
drawing in ink and tentacles.

Where her thin lips had been, a dark hole
whistled and sucked. Being young then,
I took the scene for death until I noticed
light spreading across her face, almost like joy.

3.

Anything round must be whole
and blessed. Who knows
what color to name moving water?
Does red keep, or blacken with time?

4.

You call me woman,
yet I am stronger
than you know.
You, named man,

I'm taken by your softness.
You, who are tall,
will learn what it means
to be dwarfed.

You, who are small,
will rise up
from the dark waters
where the sea and the sky merge.

BIO: AGE TEN TO FIFTY

I thought of my body at ten, slim—
And leaning into each moment
Which couldn't come fast enough,

And at twenty,
Lean and athletic—
Responsive as a violin string.

I thought of my body at thirty,
Just beginning to go soft,
How it had learned to enlarge and shrink with ease—

To carry life—how it had become protective—
Once even built a sack
Around a dying embryo.

By forty I'd come to love it for its loyalty—
Its immodest veins, rising closer and closer
To the surface.

I wondered what I would do
When it could no longer answer my demands—
No longer give me pleasure.

Fifty now, I know I would love it
Even if it were unfaithful to me—
As one day it will be.

WHY WE HAVE TWO HUNDRED PHOTOS OF ITALY AND FEW HAVE CAPTIONS

Before visiting the art museums, we walk among the Roman baths
Where couples sit on benches or stand behind monuments and kiss.
Meandering the streets of Rome, we find statues of beautiful bodies,
Breasts and penises at every turn.
Our thirteen-year-old gets an eyeful at the sidewalk magazine stands.
My husband and I strain to memorize the facts doled out at each tourist site—
But our winter was long and difficult and has left us wanting.
We are pomegranates cut open.
Every night we dine on wine and pasta and the moon.
The Mediterranean is never far away.

By the second night we know we will soon bear
The expense of a separate room for our son.
With two thousand-some lire to every one of our dollars,
Our money seems unreal anyway.
One night, when we return to our hotel and go to the office for our key,
The receptionist is making out with her boyfriend.
We are sorry for interrupting.
Next morning at breakfast, there is a fresh hickey on her neck.

I have begun to like the way the men
Let their eyes rove, taking in every detail.
At night, when I try to sleep, the brilliant purple and magenta
Bougainvillea—and the varied colors of the silk and cashmere scarves
Swirl behind my eyes. I want a scarf in every color,
And so much else I can't name.

In ancient Pompeii, it is not long before our guide
Shows us the penis etched in the sidewalk
Pointing newcomers to the brothel.
Our swirling heads wag up and down.
Of course, we say. *Of course.*

MIDLIFE INSOMNIAC

There are blue and gray undersides to black
Of course, and the long, unreasonable list
Of all that must be done immediately—
Tomorrow at the latest.
There is the warp and woof of night,
And your other career—
Studying the long list of errors
Which have aged like bad cheese.
There is the ape on the loose in the tearoom,
And the long lost lover
Who disappears when you reach for him.
There are the crippled, used years piled high,
The wise eyes you wish had never come.

You think you might make a party of it,
As long as they're staying,
Only the punch cups were lost long ago.
You'd take a hot bath
If the tub had not become the River Styx,
If Charon were not there,
Rowing steadily.
No, better to stay in bed.
He's surely on the lookout for someone—
And your strong arms,
Under the moon's fallen light, ripple.
Lovely, he might say, *come into my boat*—
And you know you wouldn't—

Couldn't

Refuse him.

LIVING IN THE KINGDOM

Something ancient is crumbling.
Birds that won't fly south
Hover outside my closed window and sing.

The house is my trap.
The cat wants to know, *What are you doing in here?*
Go outside and chase some birds.

But I don't want to chase birds.
I want them to save themselves and fly south.
I throw the cat a sock tied up with catnip.

He smiles, says, *Thanks Doll.*
I want to understand why my old ways don't work anymore—
Why things that once fascinated me bore me silly.

I want to know why my husband
Won't be bothered with me sometimes—
Why he works so much.

I want to know what could be so important you'd
Make a phone call from the top of a Ferris wheel.
(He's no doctor—nobody was dying.)

The cat lolls on his back, spread-eagled, says,
Hey Doll, cut him some slack. He's just a man,
And time's running out for him to build...

Letter from Gala to Salvador Dalí

Darling, finally I see how a pear
can become a distant hill—or an apple
buttocks. I see, too, your point about enlarging
faces while shrinking men on bicycles in the desert.
Finally I understand viewpoint—
how it can change a sofa into lips
that speak new definitions—
how objects can become almost human.

Cup and saucer, nut and bolt,
twin watches melting:
we were these things and more
until death seduced me—that ultimate assertion
against our need to complete each other.
How did you paint our separation?

And how, I beg, *should* one answer
death's bad timing?
Turn away?
Or offer a quivering hand,
despite the sudden possibilities?—
all you might have had—
all you might still have,
if not for the shadowy cloak
teasing both of your arms into
its endless tunnel of a sleeve.

In Consideration of Things

There are possessions that live longer
Than animals or humans,
Alien to everything around them.
Their purposes long forgotten,

They live out their days under my roof,
Unwelcome as squatters who pay nothing
While filling up all unused spaces.
They must have called out

To someone else
Who lived in my body once—
Called out to someone
Who loves the very

Things I despise—
(Which now litter each and every room),
Someone who hates all I
So dearly love.

When a deathly fatigue takes me under,
In a kind of near drowning,
I find that I must swim for my life
In the wake of hideous excess.

In my remade childhood,
My mother remains the librarian she always was,
Her books and call numbers giving order
To the chaotic world, her hands flying with purpose.

My father takes a different job—
At the busy corner hardware store.
They save the world, my parents:
She with her books and he with his religion,

Repair having become his sacred creed.
In the land of screws and washers,
He is a Holy Man who returns hungry each day at dusk,
Bearing light bulbs and small pieces of hardware.

Everything in our home—everything we own—works,
And he! He has lost his need for liquor while I
Want nothing more than the books Mother carries
Home in her small, grateful hands.

How We Go

Maybe the word *forever* is the one some repeat like a mantra—
The ones who appear to be moving or going on a long journey—
The ones who live by their old scouting motto: *Be prepared.*
Now they look nothing less than determined as they carry
Two bulging suitcases, a shoulder bag, a money belt, and
A passport pouch that hangs like a necklace.
The same ones are compelled to repack many times before leaving—
Rise an hour or two early even when moving from city to city,
Never mind if the roommates wake as the plastic and paper rustle,
As they fold and replace every item several times. And that innocent tone:
Am I bothering you? Did I wake you?

Some always pack light, no matter how long the trip.
Maybe they go often, so it comes easily—or
Maybe they're ever aware of that onlooker, Death.
Of course some of these must strive for their casual look,
Go to great lengths for the appearance of compactness.
And though they start out with little,
Their luggage expands with each day,
Like the base of a snowman rolled slowly downhill.
Within a couple of days they open their *Bag in a pocket.*
In go the guidebooks and memorabilia. In go
Restaurant menus and belts for brothers. In go
Scarves for sisters, and lace for grandmothers. In go
Maps and charms and leather-bound journals.

No matter how we begin, we all look about the same
Coming home: red-eyed and dazed,
Shoulders slumped in relief or defeat (we aren't sure which),
Weak smiles of pleasure at hearing English—and then, the
Sudden sadness at missing the other language.
We watch suitcases collide as they come down the chute and

Swirl on the carousel, our eyes searching for familiar markings.
Suddenly we realize that we could live forever
Without any of the things in our bags. But
Since they've traveled so far and back along with us,
We figure we might as well take them home.

WHERE GOD WAS

God was with Grandma Olson, her long
Gray hair wound into a knot at the nape of her neck.
God was in her spare living room as she rocked and
Mended our socks in her final slow days.

God was on Main Street, at the Lutheran church
Where the plump teachers—more hopeful than
My own mother—offered Bible stories and something called
Faith—all I would need for eternal salvation.

God lived in the obedient hearts of my favorite cousins,
Seeded there by their mother and father who were
Faithful always to each other—and to God too.
Jesus wanted nothing more than to see me saved—

If only I would accept his love.
But I already made a habit of saying *no*,
And Judgment Day was beyond every calendar.
I tried to hide my lack,

But my emptiness waved its red flag
Until my cousins imagined that far-off day when
They'd be in Heaven and I'd be
In Hell—or maybe Purgatory if I got lucky.

MEMORY

You tremble under the weight of all I have asked you to keep.
You want to set down your load, if only for a moment—

Or forever. I let you stop to rest.
Memory, I know you are not a horse I can whip.

I know how your back aches.
Let me bring you cool water, fine oats, a velvet blanket.

Memory, rest now.
Only promise you will rouse me

Whenever you are ready—
Day or night.

AUGUST

We rise early to beat the descending
Hands of heat. City machines
Strain to cool us—or fall eerily silent

Where the power has failed.
At 9:00 the Mexican roofers begin nailing
Dark shingles over us.

Lemonade ineffectual
Against the heat and the roof's groans.
The morning papers list the names of the young,

Next to the old, who have died.
We imagine that still moment in the future—
Interlude in our eleventh hour.

Maybe a hallucination:
Suspended in the stifling, moist air
We see something. Remnant seeds?

Seeds that might live
On if they fall
Into the sidewalk's deepest cracks.

We rise early, descend
Into the hands of heat, walk our beloved city—
Its dark alleys, its bright streets.

THE SEASON OF APPLES

When the season has passed, no amount of your good
Money can buy the sweet tartness—
Not for another full year.
And the Red Delicious apples in the grocery,
With their uniform color and shape,
Do not deliver all they promise.

You find your perfect apples
Only in late August or September:
Sour enough and not too soft—
Some scarred, carrying the warning
Graffiti of worms.

Often, things are not as they seem—
As Mona Lisa's smile was not meant
For husband or lover.
Neither was it for the juggler some thought
Had been hired to prevent
Sitting melancholy. In time, everything speaks,
Even the weak smile that comes and goes
And resembles Leonardo's.
Even the scarred apples—
The only kind you can bear to eat anymore.

MY RED CAR

Saw me in my deepest poverty
On the coldest winter nights when I placed a blanket
Over her engine before praying
She'd start the next morning so I could get to
The job that hardly paid—the one that would
Soon lead to something better. She saw
How casually I could coast into a gas station—
And how geography confused me when
I desired something I could not have—
How I would act like a homing pigeon,
Driving toward the thing I wanted,
Before turning around to go home.

My white car knew me as juggler, saw
How I could steer while at the same time digging below
The seat for a can leaking the final droplets of apple juice—
How I could listen to radio news
While offering the words for a song or rhyme.
Saw how I could make a wide turn while soothing a sick child.
Saw how I sat on cracker crumbs without care, and even happily
Ground them deeper into the seats stained with crayon scribbles.
The white one saw how I made a habit of bringing a banana along,
That easy fruit that staves off hunger—and how I kept on
Even after one got smashed into the carpeting.

My black car saw my fear—when we found
Her burned out in the bad neighborhood where we'd left her,
Before the Twins' seventh playoff game. She saw how quickly
I assigned her devastation to vandals—and wondered, too,
If it could be a sign from God—
Until days later, when the report came
Laying blame on the stuck seat motor.
She saw how I could be lured into a world of false assumptions.

My tan car saw my toughness. How once
I kept driving even after a tire had gone completely flat
And begun smoking and reeking of burned metal.
She saw me as scavenger, mind veering, choosing
Other routes though already overdue somewhere.
She understood how I'd come to know the city so well:
By default, same as I'd come by so much else.
She told no one though, except the other cars, so that together
They knew more about me than I knew about myself.

Ars Poetica

Poetry is the thick rope I cling to at the hospital.
It is the good doctor who loves all his patients.
It is the minister's smile telling us to go on,
the teacher's star of approval,
the plumber's wrench,
the squirrel's nut.
It loves both sinner and saint in each of us.
It walks us through the deep woods of despair and
leads us into a clearing, where it feeds
us sunshine again,
then gives us a new name for the sun,
then turns again to rope,
to minister, to teacher.

NOTES

"Chant of the School Lunch Ladies": On October 28, 2003, fifteen cooks and one janitor from the elementary school in Holdingford, Minnesota, together turned in their winning lottery ticket purchased from a pool to which each had been contributing. With a winning $95.5 million, each winner had the choice of receiving $2.1 million in cash or annual payments of about $134,000 for 30 years.

"Letter from Gala to Salvador Dalí": Elena Diakonova, known as Gala, left the French poet, Paul Éluard, to live with painter Salvador Dalí. Some believe that Gala saved Dalí from serious nervous disorientation, and that she helped him to become successful by taking charge of his life. Dalí is perhaps best known for his surrealistic works. After Gala's death in 1982, he lived for several more years, until 1989. There are large Salvador Dalí museums in Figueres, Spain, and St. Petersburg, Florida.

After a childhood on the North Dakota prairie, MARY L. JUNGE lives and writes in the Twin Cities, Minnesota. A teacher, mother, and grandmother, she has studied writing with numerous instructors from the Loft, a center for writing in Minneapolis, and the Iowa Summer Writing Festival. Junge has also benefited from writing residencies at Norcroft, Minnesota, and Ragdale, Illinois. Her poems have been published in a variety of literary journals; her personal essays and articles have appeared in local, national, and international publications. Junge's poem "Demerol Dreams" was nominated for a 2001 Pushcart Prize. *Express Train*, a chapbook, was published by Pudding House Publications in 2002.

L A U R E L
P O E T R Y
COLLECTIVE

A gathering of twenty-three poets and graphic artists living in the Twin Cities area, the Laurel Poetry Collective is a collaboration dedicated to publishing beautiful and affordable books, chap-books, and broadsides. Started in 2002, its four-year charter is to publish and celebrate, one by one, a book or chapbook by each of its twenty-one poet members. The Laurel members are: Lisa Ann Berg, Teresa Boyer, Annie Breitenbucher, Margot Fortunato Galt, Georgia A. Greeley, Ann Iverson, Mary L. Junge, Deborah Keenan, Joyce Kennedy, Ilze Kļaviņa Mueller, Yvette Nelson, Eileen O'Toole, Kathy Alma Peterson, Regula Russelle, Sylvia Ruud, Tom Ruud, Su Smallen, Susanna Styve, Suzanne Swanson, Nancy M. Walden, Lois Welshons, Pam Wynn, Nolan Zavoral.

For current information about the series—including broadsides, subscriptions, and single copy purchase—visit:

www.laurelpoetry.com

or write:

Laurel Poetry Collective
1168 Laurel Avenue
St. Paul, MN 55104